THE CRUCIBLE OF THE CHRISTIAN LANTERN

(Marriage)

By Colette Ajoku

"But may the God of all grace, who called us to His eternal glory by Christ Jesus, after you have suffered a while, perfect, establish, strengthen, and settle you."

1 Peter 5:10 (NKJV)

COPYRIGHT

Cover design: *Colette Ajoku*
Layout: *WDK Studios*
First Edition, 2025

For more information, ministry inquiries, or speaking engagements:
coletteajoku@gmail.com
Instagram: @coletteajoku
Impactville

ISBN: 978-978-691-982-9
Published by: ChoWilson.com
7, Agboga Boulevard, Rose Garden Estate,
Isashi, Lagos, Nigeria

AUTHOR'S NOTE

This book was born out of prayer. In the quiet, refining seasons where words are fewer, and God's whispers are louder. Through personal encounters with God's refining grace. Each page reflects lessons learned in love, surrender, and faith. It came through the moments when love was tested, patience stretched, and faith purified in the fire of surrender.

Marriage is a divine classroom, and in it, God does not simply join two people; He refines two hearts. Through joy and conflict, silence and laughter, misunderstanding and mercy, He burns away self so that His love can remain. Every lesson in these pages was first lived, sometimes painfully, but always under the tender eye of a faithful God. I have learned that grace is not only the oil that keeps the flame burning, but also the fire that purifies the vessel.

My prayer for you, dear reader, is simple: As you walk through your own crucible, you will not resist the refining work of God. Your heart will be strengthened, and your light rekindled, for the God who refines will also restore. You will see His purpose in the process, and you will trust the One who called you to this covenant, for He will complete what He began. So when the fire cools, and the smoke clears, may you find that your lantern still burns brighter, purer, and filled with the light of His love.

Colette Ajoku

DEDICATION

To God Almighty,
the Refiner of my soul,
the Light in every lantern,
and the Keeper of every covenant.

To the One who perfects all things concerning us.

ACKNOWLEDGMENTS

Gratitude fills every page of this book because it was never written alone.

To my beloved husband, **Ken Ajoku**, thank you for being my covering, my confidant, and my constant companion through every season of life and faith. Your patience, wisdom, and unwavering devotion have been living proof that God still refines through love. You have stood beside me through fire and stillness, teaching me daily what humility, strength, and godly leadership look like. This book carries your quiet prayers, your steadfast encouragement, and your fingerprints of faith on every page. I thank God for you, not only as my husband, but as my partner in destiny, ministry, and divine purpose.

To our three precious children -**Nedu, Chiso, and Chimmy**- you are my greatest earthly treasures and daily reflections of God's faithfulness. Your laughter fills our home with joy, your prayers strengthen my spirit, and your love reminds me of the simple beauty of grace. You are each a bright flame in our family's lantern of faith.

To my twin sister, **Chinelo Nzeaka,** thank you for being a lifelong reflection of encouragement, laughter, and prayer. Your heart, your faith, and your unwavering support have been both anchor and mirror. You have stood with me in every season, a true twin flame of purpose and grace.

To my siblings, each uniquely gifted and dearly loved, thank you for standing beside me through life's seasons with laughter, honesty, and encouragement. Your support and faith have been quiet pillars behind my journey. You are living reminders that family is one of God's greatest expressions of love.

To my beloved parents, **Engr. Luke and Bertha Obi**, thank you for laying the foundation of my faith and for modeling devotion, diligence, and enduring love. Your lives are a testimony of what it means to walk with God with steadfast hearts. Every prayer you prayed, every sacrifice you made, and every word of wisdom you spoke still echoes in my life.

To my dear parents-in-law, **Mr. Jonathan and Cecelia Ajoku**, thank you for embracing me with love, wisdom, and kindness. Your prayers, encouragement, and godly example have been a quiet strength in our family's journey.

To my dear **Pastor Love Mii** and **Pastor Niyi**, the **Weight Lifting Team**, who saw what God is stirring inside, encouraged me in the Word and prayed this book into reality. To my **Sonship prayer sisters**. To my dear **Rev. Oyiks Alfred**, under whose teaching and guidance I sat for years and have enjoyed the privilege to serve in the women's ministry. I thank God for the grace to serve in the children's ministry, the choir, and the youth ministry. Each ministry experience built in me deeper faith, courage, and perseverance, which are living illustrations of God's transforming grace. You all remind me that the Church is not a place, but a people filled with the fire and light of Christ.

To every young or old, single, engaged, married, divorced, or widowed believer who has walked through the fires of love and life, your courage to believe again has inspired these words. Your stories remind me that God never wastes pain, and that every crucible still carries the possibility of light.

And finally, to the **Holy Spirit, my Teacher, Comforter, and Co-Author,** thank You for every whisper of wisdom, every flame of revelation, and every breath of grace that shaped this book. Without

You, these words would be empty; with You, they carry eternal life and light.

With love, gratitude, and reverence,

Colette Ajoku
Intercessor | Wife of One | Mother of Three | Servant of Grace

---

FOREWORD

When Colette first shared the vision for The Crucible of the Christian Lantern, I witnessed the birth of a work shaped not only by words but by prayer, perseverance, and the quiet strength that defines her life. As her husband, I have seen firsthand the refining fires she writes about, moments of joy and challenge, laughter and silence, faith, and surrender. This book is not just a collection of lessons; it is a living testimony of grace at work in our home.

Colette's journey has been marked by a deep commitment to God, to our marriage, and to the calling of the family and marriage ministry. Her wisdom is not theoretical; it is lived, sometimes painfully, but always stands the test of time. Through seasons of testing, she has shown me that love is not simply a feeling, but a covenant that endures and transforms. Her prayers have been the quiet covering over me, our children, extended family members, and loved ones. Her encouragement has been a steady anchor in times of uncertainty.

She has taught me that marriage is not about perfection, though we strive for excellence through Christ, but it is more about persistence, genuine care, and concern. Not about winning but about worshipping together through every trial and success. The lessons here are the ones we have learned side by side, always under the watchful eye of a faithful God.

There are so many moments that come to mind, but a few stand out as milestones in our journey. I remember the early days of our marriage, when we were still learning how to blend two worlds into one. There were times when we disagreed over trivial things, perhaps how to handle a family situation or a decision about our children. The tension could linger longer than either of us wanted. More often than you would expect, we would always find a middle ground, where we would allow God to speak to our hearts and humble us. Instead of letting pride win, Colette and I would quietly reach for each other's hands, smile, and pray together. I still remember one of her prayers, "Lord, teach us to see each other through Your eyes. Let this situation refine us, not divide us." It wasn't always an instant fix, but it is a lesson that the Crucible is not a place of defeat, but of transformation.

To our three lovely children, **Nedu, Chiso, and Chimmy,** you are the living proof of the light Colette carries. Your laughter fills our home, your prayers strengthen our spirits, and your love reminds us daily of God's faithfulness and love.

As you read these pages, you will encounter the heart of a woman who believes that marriage is a divine classroom, where God refines two hearts for His glory. You will find love, honesty, hope, and the gentle reminder that the same fire that tests also purifies. She invites you to embrace the process, to trust the Refiner, and to discover that after the fire, there is still grace.

It is my honor to stand beside Colette not only as her husband but as her partner in destiny, ministry, and purpose. I pray that this book will rekindle your faith, strengthen your love, and remind you that the God who refines will also restore.

With gratitude and love,

Ken Ajoku

ENDORSEMENTS

Wow, this is deeply rich. This is a book everyone (single or married) needs to read and digest. It has a lot of healthy nuggets that are strong and direct. The part I love the most is the quote below. "Marriage: The Reflection of Christ and His Church. There was already a divine blueprint before there was Adam and Eve, a heavenly pattern of love between Christ and His Church. Marriage on earth is not merely a union of two people; it is a reflection of a greater mystery, the relationship between the Redeemer and the redeemed." What a revelation? No wonder Paul also wrote "husbands love your wives as Christ loves the church" It's truly about "The Redeemer and The Redeemed" God bless you for putting this together.

Pastor Olugbenga Olumuyiwa

This book might be our AMEN to what seems to be a big time deficit in understanding and appreciation of what marriage is meant to be: started with desire, strengthened by covenant love and divine design... beyond emotions, grounded in God's purpose ... partnership beyond convenience ... a crucible refining the individual and couple for excellence! It is an important read for those contemplating, for those preparing, and for those married. I look forward to getting my copy of the book.

Mrs Idowu Okunzua

The Crucible of the Christian Lantern: Marriage is a profound exploration of God's design for marriage as a living reflection of Christ and His church. In the crucible of trials, couples discover that forgiveness is not merely a virtue but the very heartbeat of redemption—"In him we have redemption through his blood, the forgiveness of our trespasses, according to the riches of his grace" (Ephesians 1:7). This book illuminates how a "crucible marriage" refines both partners, forging authentic growth, resilience, and grace that mirrors Christ Himself.

Minister Chinenye Okonkwo

It is a VERY INSTRUCTIVE AND CONCISE DELIVERY OF THE DIVINE PURPOSE OF MARRIAGE. Honestly, you've done well.

Mr Uchenna Nzeaka

This book, "The Crucible of the Christian Lantern: Marriage," is a deeply needed, Spirit-led book that brings believers back to God's original blueprint for covenant love. With biblical truth and heartfelt wisdom, Colette Ajoku shows how God uses the trials of marriage to refine, restore, and reveal His glory. I have been married for 26 years and still find this book fascinating. I wholeheartedly endorse this work and recommend it to every couple, every pastor, counselor, and every believer seeking God's purpose for marriage.

Elder Monday Mii

"The Crucible of the Christian Lantern: Marriage" shared biblical insights while illuminating with honesty the joys, tests, and transformative power of a Christ-centred union. A deeply enriching read for couples seeking to build a marriage anchored in purpose, faith, and grace.

Pastor Rolayo Akhigbe

This book is a bomb!!!

I have just gone through this amazing book, "THE CRUCIBLE OF THE CHRISTIAN LANTERN."

What a bomb! What a book! This book has Spirit and power resting on it. In this book is the power to restore, heal, and teach love. I would recommend this book to every married couple, irrespective of how long you have been married, and to every intended couple. Read it before your wedding.

What a Blessing!!

Pastor Chinyere Isibor

The wisdom shared in the book is unparalleled and definitely inspired by the Holy Spirit. Having been married for 40 years, I wholeheartedly support Colette's statement that: In God's design, marriage is not about two people completing or complementing each other; rather, it is about them conforming to Christ.

Dr. Shola Omidiran

PREFACE

Writing and documenting have always been my peaceful place. Precious moments where my thoughts find order and my heart finds calm. Friends often tease me by calling me "the scribe," and perhaps rightly so. There's something sacred about putting on paper the words God whispers in quiet moments. The inspiration for The Crucible of the Christian Lantern came in a dream. At first, the phrase made no sense, but as I prayed, the Lord unfolded its meaning. He showed me that every Christian life and marriage is refined in the crucible, first tested by fire, yet made to shine brighter through grace.

The Book of Psalms deeply influenced this journey too because its honest expressions of worship and sorrow taught me that it is possible to bring every feeling before God, whether joy, pain, or longing, and still find peace in His presence.

Much of what I share also flows from my marriage journey; the laughter, the lessons, and the refining moments that deepened my understanding of love and faith. The example of my parents' marriage reinforced those truths, showing me that commitment and grace hold a home together.

I hope these pages will speak to hearts walking through their own refining fires, and remind each reader that God's love still burns steadily, even in the crucible.

Colette Ajoku

CONTENTS

INTRODUCTION - DEFINING MARRIAGE AND THE CRUCIBLE

Marriage is one of the most sacred covenants ever entrusted to humanity. It is a divine partnership designed not simply for companionship, but for transformation. In a world that often celebrates love without responsibility and emotion without endurance, the Christian marriage stands as a living altar where two lives are refined by grace and tested by truth. I learnt this through my journey of the Crucible.

When God joins two people, He doesn't merely combine personalities or plans; He forges purpose. Every covenant union becomes a *crucible,* a sacred vessel where heat is applied, impurities are removed, and what remains is purer, stronger, and more reflective of His image. Are you about to enter this phase?

A crucible is not a place of destruction, but of purification. It is where gold is tested, where iron is strengthened, and where what is genuine endures. The marriage covenant functions in much the same way because it exposes weaknesses, demands surrender, and invites the Holy Spirit to shape love into something eternal.

For many couples, including my husband and me, the first years of marriage reveal how inadequate human strength alone truly is. Love feels fragile, expectations clash, and self rises to defend its comfort. But remember, even in conflict, God is refining character, teaching humility, and deepening dependence on Him. You must understand that the same fire that tests is also the fire that purifies.

Scripture tells us:

"In this you greatly rejoice, though now for a little while, if need be, you have been grieved by various trials, that the genuineness of your faith, being much more precious than gold that perishes, though it is tested by fire, may be found to praise, honor, and glory at the revelation of Jesus Christ."

1 Peter 1:6-7

Marriage, then, is not the absence of trials; rather, it is the presence of grace amid trials. God uses this covenant to expose what cannot endure and to strengthen what must remain. Every misunderstanding, disappointment, or delay becomes an invitation to trust His process rather than our feelings.

And just as Peter reminds us in his letter:

"But may the God of all grace, who called us to His eternal glory by Christ Jesus, after you have suffered a while, perfect, establish, strengthen, and settle you."

1 Peter 5:10

The refining does not last forever because the God who allows the testing also promises restoration. He perfects, strengthens, and settles those who remain yielded. So, as you read this book, approach it not as a manual on marriage alone, but as a mirror of faith. Every single page draws your eyes away from your spouse and toward your Savior, yes, the true Bridegroom, who refines in love and restores by grace. If your marriage feels like a crucible, please take heart, you are not being consumed, you are being transformed.

Be assured that when the refining is complete, your union will shine with a light that points back to the One who ordained it. GOD.

Part One: The Refining
IGNITED

CHAPTER 1 - THE CRUCIBLE AND THE COVENANT

Marriage did not begin with man's idea but with God's intention.

Defining Marriage: God's Original Design

From the very beginning, the Lord set marriage within His creative order, a divine covenant meant to reveal His heart.

> ***"Therefore a man shall leave his father and mother and be joined to his wife, and they shall become one flesh."***
>
> ***Genesis 2:24***

In that first union, God showed that love is not merely attraction but assignment. Marriage is holy ground. It is a partnership built on obedience, not convenience. Sadly, when couples forget this, they treat the covenant as a contract. A covenant is not a contract, and covenant love does not end when conditions change; it endures because God Himself sustains it.

God's Design, Not Our Desire

Every believer must understand this truth: marriage is God's design, not our desire.

Desire may draw two hearts together, but design keeps them standing when the storms come.

A marriage founded solely on emotion or personal happiness becomes fragile and easily shaken once expectations fail. But when it is grounded in God's purpose, it gains divine stability.

Sadly, our desires are often short-sighted, but God's design is very eternal.

He sees that we need to grow in character, patience, and holiness even when it is uncomfortable. On my marriage journey, I learnt that you cannot build what you did not create because God creates, God designs, therefore God builds.

"Unless the Lord builds the house, they labor in vain who build it."

Psalm 127:1a

In God's design, marriage is not about completing each other but about conforming to Christ.

It is not about finding someone who meets your every need but becoming someone who reflects His nature, which is why the greatest mistake many couples make is building on desire instead of divine order, because desire will fail you. When feelings fade as they always do, only design sustains.

When we return to His blueprint, we discover that the purpose of marriage is not to make us comfortable, but to make us Christlike, and to make heaven.

Desire gives pleasure; design gives purpose, and only purpose can endure the fire.

Marriage: The Reflection of Christ and His Church

There was already a divine blueprint before there was Adam and Eve, a heavenly pattern of love between Christ and His Church.

God himself designed marriage to reflect this relationship: the marriage of Christ and His Bride (the Church), the blueprint which divinely existed before the foundation of the world.

Marriage on earth is not merely a union of two people; it is a reflection of a greater mystery, the relationship between the Redeemer and the redeemed.

"For this reason a man shall leave his father and mother and be joined to his wife, and the two shall become one flesh. This is a great mystery, but I speak concerning Christ and the church."

Ephesians 5:31-32

From the beginning, God intended marriage to mirror His own covenant of love, which is sacrificial, steadfast, and sanctifying. In the love between husband and wife, He chose to display His tenderness,

His patience, and His pursuit.

When a woman honors her husband with trust and reverence, she mirrors the Church's response to her Lord: humble, devoted, and obedient in love. When a man loves his wife with grace, he echoes Christ's love for the Church, a love that serves, covers, and forgives.

This is why we cannot treat marriage lightly. It is not only a covenant of companionship; it is a living sermon of redemption.

Every act of forgiveness preaches the cross.

Every reconciliation reveals resurrection.

Every enduring union whispers to the world, "Christ still loves His bride."

The crucible of marriage, therefore, is not punishment; it is participation in God's design.

God purifies both hearts through the refining fires of relationship so that His image is seen more clearly. To love well is to worship, to forgive freely is to minister, and to remain faithful in fire is to reveal Christ.

The Meaning of the Crucible

A crucible is a vessel that holds intense heat to refine metal until impurities rise and purity remains. In the same way, marriage is God's refining vessel where two hearts are melted together and shaped into one.

1 Peter 1:6-7 declares,

"... though now for a little while, if need be, you have been grieved by various trials, that the genuineness of your faith, being much more precious than gold that perishes, though it is tested by fire, may be found to praise, honor, and glory at the revelation of Jesus Christ."

The fire of marriage is not sent to destroy love but to reveal its quality. God allows heat, which can come in the form of misunderstandings, pressure, or disappointments, so that pride burns away and purity remains.

The Significance of the Christian Lantern

From this book's title, The Crucible of the Christian Lantern, the crucible represents the refining, and the lantern represents the believer, the vessel carrying God's light through that refining.

Every Christian home is called to be a lantern: a light shining in a dark world, fueled by the oil of grace and guarded by the glass of godly character.

Jesus said in ***Matthew 5:14-16,***

"You are the light of the world. A city that is set on a hill cannot be hidden. Nor do they light a lamp and put it under a basket, but on a lampstand, and it gives light to all who are in the house. Let your light so shine before men, that they may see your good works and glorify your Father in heaven."

In marriage, this light is tested in the crucible, not to be extinguished, but to be made purer and brighter, so when the couple endures refining together, their flame becomes steady, and it burns not with passion alone, but with purpose.

The Christian lantern is not self-lit; its flame comes from the Spirit of God, and prayer is its oil, obedience its wick, and unity the glass that protects the flame from being quenched by offense or pride.

Without the crucible, the lantern's flame flickers, but within the crucible, the flame matures; it no longer burns wildly, but wisely.

So, when you walk through trials, remember that God is not trying to put out your light; He is teaching you how to burn steadily. Your marriage becomes the light by which the world sees Jesus, and the hotter the crucible, the brighter the light will shine.

The Process of Refinement

Refinement in marriage looks different for every couple. Sometimes it comes through financial strain, health challenges, or seasons of silence, and many times from family members. Yet every trial holds one invitation: to yield to God's work instead of resisting it.

1 Peter 5:10 promises,

"But may the God of all grace, who called us to His eternal glory by Christ Jesus, after you have suffered a while, perfect, establish, strengthen, and settle you."

If both husband and wife allow God to do the work, the outcome is stability and peace. Always keep this in mind: the crucible may be hot, but it is also holy.

When Love Meets Fire

In the early months of marriage, couples often discover that passion alone is not enough to keep the peace.

Little habits once overlooked now feel irritating, and expectations clash with reality.

This is where many begin to wonder if they made the right choice.

Yes, I wondered too, but the truth is simple: passion must translate into covenant love, which is evidenced by commitment.

Emotions can start marriages; covenant sustains them.

Romans 5:3-4 remind us,

"... we also glory in tribulations, knowing that tribulation produces perseverance; and perseverance, character; and character, hope."

When couples persevere through friction, they find deeper unity not because it is easy, but because grace has taught them endurance.

Letting Go and Letting God

The theme of this book, **"Let Go, Let God,"** begins right here.

The crucible demands surrender. We cannot hold on to pride, control, or fear and still expect transformation.

When we let go of our way, God begins to shape something new. When we invite Him into the heat, He turns fire into formation.

Every time we choose prayer over panic and surrender over stubbornness, we invite heaven into the marriage.

The crucible becomes the classroom where we learn holiness through humility.

Reflection Moment

"Lord, have we built our marriage on Your design or our desires? Are we protecting the light You placed within us?"

Father, help us remember that our home is Your lantern. Align our hearts with Your design. Teach us to see marriage the way You see it, not as a place to be pleased, but as a place to be purified. Keep our flame from flickering in the heat of life. May the fire that refines us never destroy us, but purify our love so it reflects You more clearly.

CHAPTER 2 - THE ASSIGNMENT OF FIRE

Every marriage begins with light.

The vows are said, the prayers are prayed, and the future feels full of endless peace. You look at each other and think, *We'll never be like those couples who fight.*

And then life begins to unfold.

The First Sparks of Reality

In the early seasons of marriage, love feels effortless. At least that was our thought because of how young and ignorant we were. I always smile at the memory.

There are long talks, laughter over little things, and dreams that feel within reach, but as time passes, something sacred happens: **the testing begins.**

Every marriage will face moments where love meets fire, not because God is cruel, but because He is committed to growth. The same love that felt light in courtship feels heavy in covenant. Some courtships are smooth, while some hint at the journey ahead. In the covenant, the responsibilities, personalities, and pressures clash, and suddenly, emotion alone can no longer sustain what must now be built by faith.

"Beloved, do not think it strange concerning the fiery trial which is to try you, as though some strange thing happened to you."

1 Peter 4:12

God allows the flame not to burn us, but to burn away what keeps His glory from being seen through us.

The Collision of Two Worlds

Marriage brings two different worlds into one space. Two ways of thinking, feeling, and reacting.

At first, the differences feel exciting, but later, they can feel exhausting.

It is here that irritation replaces infatuation. The small habits once overlooked now seem magnified. Arguments arise over tone, timing, and trivial things. Many couples think something has gone wrong, but nothing has.

This is simply the refining stage. **The crucible has been lit.**

What you're feeling is not failure, it is formation.

"As iron sharpens iron, so a man sharpens the countenance of his friend."

Proverbs 27:17

God uses your spouse not to frustrate you, but to form you. Your spouse is not your enemy.

Your spouse reveals the places in your heart that need grace, humility, and healing.

The Potter's Purpose Behind the Pressure

Pressure is not punishment; it is purpose. Without it, gold remains hidden beneath dross.

Every disagreement, every disappointment, every unmet expectation is an invitation to grow in grace.

Instead of asking, "Why is this happening?" we must begin to ask, "What is God refining in me through this?"

When I channeled my questions rightly, things began to make sense and to change.

Romans 8:28 reminds us,

"And we know that all things work together for good to those who love God, to those who are the called according to His purpose."

The testing is not random; it is orchestrated by a loving Father who wants to produce something eternal.

When we yield to the process, the fire becomes a friend, shaping character, deepening love, and purifying motives.

When Love Feels Like Work

The early feelings of romance were the seed; now comes the cultivation, and cultivation demands your participation, your commitment, and your sweat.

Love that once flowed naturally must now be chosen intentionally. You have to apologize when you feel right. You need to forgive when it still hurts. And you will have to pray when you feel tired. True love is not proven in passion but in perseverance.

"Love suffers long and is kind; love does not envy; love does not parade itself, is not puffed up."

1 Corinthians 13:4

The fire exposes selfishness and calls forth sacrifice. It teaches us that love is not always soft. Sometimes, it is strong.

Sometimes, it chooses to stay when everything human wants to leave.

The Refining of Faith Through Surrender

Faith is the foundation of the covenant.

When the fire intensifies, many try to fix each other, but the call is to return to faith. You might wonder why. It is because you cannot change your spouse through pressure, but you can invite God through prayer. Faith anchors love when emotions fluctuate. It reminds you that God is still working, even in silence.

Hebrews 10:36 says,

"For you have need of endurance, so that after you have done the will of God, you may receive the promise."

The refining of faith within marriage turns temporary affection into a lasting covenant. Faith says, "God, even when I don't see change, I will still trust Your process."

Letting God Be Lord in the Fire

In every refining season, there comes a moment of surrender, when both partners must decide whether God will simply be part of the marriage or Lord over it. When He is Lord, we stop trying to win arguments and start working for peace. We stop competing for control and start partnering in prayer. We stop trying to fix our spouse and start letting Him fix us. The fire is safest when God is the one holding it.

Isaiah 43:2b promises,

"When you walk through the fire, you shall not be burned, nor shall the flame scorch you."

When Christ reigns at the center, even the hottest fire cannot consume you; it will only consume what doesn't belong in you.

Reflection Moment

"Lord, what are You revealing about Yourself through the heat we are walking through?"

Father, help us not to fear the fire but to trust its purpose. Teach us to see each other through Your eyes when the heat rises. May our love be refined, our faith deepened, and our light never dimmed.

CHAPTER 3 - THE UNSEEN BATTLE: RECOGNIZING THE REAL ENEMY

The Spiritual Reality of Marriage

Every marriage is a spiritual battlefield long before it becomes a physical or emotional one.

The covenant of marriage reflects the relationship between Christ and His Church, and because of that, it will always attract spiritual resistance.

"For we do not wrestle against flesh and blood, but against principalities, against powers, against the rulers of the darkness of this age, against spiritual hosts of wickedness in the heavenly places."

Ephesians 6:12

When couples lose sight of this truth, they fight the wrong battles, turning against each other instead of standing together. The enemy's greatest strategy is division, because he knows that unity carries divine power. Marriage is not just a partnership. **Marriage is an altar,** and wherever there is an altar, there will always be opposition.

When the Enemy Shifts the Focus

The devil is subtle.

He rarely appears with horns and fire; instead, he whispers. Watch out for those whispers because they have destroyed homes. The devil whispers suspicion, resentment, fear, and offense. He wants couples to focus on each other's weaknesses rather than on God's faithfulness. He knows that if he can turn the couple against each other, their prayers will lose agreement and therefore, power.

"And if a house is divided against itself, that house cannot stand."

Mark 3:25

The enemy doesn't need to destroy the home; he only needs to disrupt its peace. He doesn't have to silence prayer; he only has to introduce pride. He doesn't have to end love; he only has to erode trust. As Apostle Arome Osayi notes in Decimating Demonic Devices, "Demons are intelligent beings." They study patterns, exploit weaknesses, and whisper words of offense and pride. Their strategy is not always destruction; it is often division. When couples cannot discern this, they direct their anger at each other instead of the real adversary. The unseen battle is not against personality but against principality.

"Lest Satan should take advantage of us; for we are not ignorant of his devices."

2 Corinthians 2:11

This is why spiritual awareness is vital, because you cannot win a war you don't know you're in.

Standing United in Warfare

Every couple must learn to recognize spiritual warfare, not with fear, but with faith.

When disagreements arise, **step back and ask:**

"Is this really us, or is this an attack meant to divide us?" From my experience, the enemy introduces disagreements when the Lord is about to open a spiritual door of growth. I learnt with time by being more spiritually aware. Prayer is the first defense. Unity is the second. When a husband and wife pray together, the power of agreement dismantles the plans of darkness. When they forgive quickly, the door of offense stays closed. And when they walk in humility, grace flows freely.

James 4:7 teaches,

"Therefore submit to God. Resist the devil and he will flee from you."

The important word here is submit, not just resist. Spiritual authority flows from surrender. When the marriage submits to God's order, the enemy loses access.

The Power of Agreement

The most underestimated weapon in a Christian marriage is agreement.

Jesus said,

"Again I say to you that if two of you agree on earth concerning anything that they ask, it will be done for them by My Father in heaven."

Matthew 18:19

Agreement brings divine acceleration, but where there is strife, progress slows.

Therefore, the enemy works hard to plant small seeds of discord, silent assumptions, harsh tones, and emotional withdrawal. He knows that the moment you lose agreement, your prayer loses alignment.

Guard your unity as fiercely as you guard your love. Pray together even when it feels awkward.

Speak blessings even when emotions are raw because agreement doesn't always begin in feeling; it begins in faith.

Learning to See Beyond the Natural

Spiritual maturity means learning to see through, not just see at. When tempers rise or disappointments deepen, pause and look beyond what's visible.

Ask the Holy Spirit for discernment:

"Lord, what's really happening here? Is there a deeper battle beneath this moment?" God often reveals that the issue isn't just miscommunication or emotion, but distraction. The enemy distracts through constant irritation, so that couples stop focusing on purpose and start focusing on pain. Once you discern this pattern, you can choose peace over pride and prayer over argument.

2 Corinthians 2:11 warns,

"Lest Satan should take advantage of us; for we are not ignorant of his devices."

The more you understand his tactics, the less power he has over your home.

Peace as a Weapon

In the natural realm, peace feels passive, but in the Spirit, peace is powerful. Every time you refuse to retaliate, you disarm the enemy. Every time you choose patience, you reinforce victory.

Romans 16:20a declares,

"And the God of peace will crush Satan under your feet shortly."

Did you notice that word, **God of Peace**? It is not the God of war, but the God of peace, that will crush the enemy. Peace confuses the darkness because it shows the devil that he no longer controls your reactions.

Keep your home soaked in worship, prayer, and gratitude. This is a big weapon.

Keep in mind that peace is not the absence of trouble, but the presence of trust.

The Marriage that Stands Together

When couples understand the real enemy, their posture changes.

They stop accusing and start interceding. They stop shouting and start standing.

And they stop seeing each other as the opposition and start seeing each other as allies.

The fire becomes a place of unity, not division, and the crucible becomes the ground where victory is forged because no weapon formed against a praying marriage can prosper.

"Though one may be overpowered by another, two can withstand him. And a threefold cord is not quickly broken."

Ecclesiastes 4:12

When the husband and wife stand together with Christ as the third strand, **hell trembles.**

Reflection Moment

Have we been fighting the wrong battles? Have we allowed the enemy to turn us against each other?" Ask the Holy Spirit to show you where the real battle lies. Is it pride? Fear? Misunderstanding? Outside influence?

Then, take your spouse's hand, literally or in prayer, and say aloud:

"Teach us to recognize the real enemy and to stand in unity. Let Your peace rule in our hearts and our home. We are not each other's enemy, and we stand together in Jesus' name." Watch peace return to your home.

CHAPTER 4 - THE REFINING OF CHARACTER

For every heart in the fire of transformation, may you see God's hand in the heat.

The Fire That Reveals, Not Destroys

Every marriage, no matter how strong or tender, will face a moment when God turns up the heat not to destroy, but to reveal. The refining fire exposes what smooth days often hide: pride, impatience, hidden expectations, and unhealed wounds.

When those things surface, it can feel like failure, but really, the Refiner is drawing impurities to the surface so that love can become pure again.

> ***"He will sit as a refiner and a purifier of silver; He will purify the sons of Levi, and purge them as gold and silver, that they may offer to the Lord an offering in righteousness."***
>
> *Malachi 3:3*

The fire is measured because God knows how much heat your heart can handle, and He never leaves the crucible unattended.

Sometimes, in my marriage, the very argument I wanted to escape became the place where God showed me myself: my tone, my impatience, my need to win.

When I surrendered that moment, peace began to return.

Marriage: God's Mirror of the Heart

Marriage doesn't just reveal who our spouse is; it reveals who we still are. Every exchange, every irritation, every silence becomes a mirror, and God asks softly, "Can you see what I'm showing you about you?"

"As in water face reflects face, so a man's heart reveals the man."

Proverbs 27:19

In those reflections, if we are humble enough to admit it, we see both our weaknesses and His grace.

The mirror doesn't condemn, it reveals, and it corrects.

The mirror invites us to let the Holy Spirit reshape our reactions, our expectations, our speech, and when we let Him, the same mirror that once showed flaws begins to reflect His image.

Fruit of the Spirit Meets the Fire

Everyone loves to quote Galatians 5, but few realize where the fruit grows.

Love grows where forgiveness is tested. Joy blooms where comfort is absent. Peace takes root in tension.

"But the fruit of the Spirit is love, joy, peace, longsuffering, kindness, goodness, faithfulness, gentleness, self-control."

Galatians 5:22-23

Sometimes I've prayed, "Lord, make me patient," and then found myself in seasons that tried every ounce of patience I thought I had. That's how fruit ripens, not in theory, but in testing, so the next time the fire flares, remember: God is answering prayers you have already prayed.

He is growing the fruit you asked for.

The Weight of Humility

Humility is the posture that keeps us steady in the fire.

Without it, every correction feels like an accusation, and pain can teach the wrong lessons. When one partner chooses humility, it changes the atmosphere of the home.

Sometimes one gentle apology can silence a thousand accusations.

I've seen it in my life and in the lives of others I've prayed with and counseled. When one person bows, heaven steps in.

"Therefore humble yourselves under the mighty hand of God, that He may exalt you in due time."

1 Peter 5:6

Humility does not mean weakness; it means surrendered strength. Strength submitted to God.

The moment you stop defending your pride, God begins defending your peace.

Grace for Growth, Not Perfection

Refinement isn't about perfection, but about progress.

God is not after that spotless performance; He is after a surrendered heart. Will you fail sometimes? A big YES! You will even say things you regret, things you wish you had prayed about sooner, but grace remains the atmosphere where growth happens.

"... My grace is sufficient for you, for My strength is made perfect in weakness."

2 Corinthians 12:9a

When we allow grace to meet our weakness, transformation begins quietly, one surrendered response at a time.

Even our stumbles can become stepping stones when offered back to Him.

The Gift of Refinement

Refinement is God's love in its most honest form.

He removes what hinders so that His likeness can shine through. It may feel painful, but it is purifying you for something weightier, peace that lasts, joy that stays, love that endures.

"But may the God of all grace, who called you to His eternal glory by Christ Jesus, after you have suffered a while, perfect, establish, strengthen, and settle you."

1 Peter 5:10

What the fire removes is temporary, but what it leaves is eternal.

Every time you choose forgiveness over resentment, you are becoming more like Jesus. Every time you choose prayer over pride, you are protecting the flame within.

The fire is not against you; the fire is for you. And when it's over, you'll recognize yourself in His reflection.

Reflection Moment

"What has marriage revealed in me that I didn't see before? Am I allowing the fire to refine me, or am I resisting it?"

Lord, thank You for loving me enough to refine me. Help me see the beauty in what You are burning away. Give me humility to learn, patience to grow, and grace to endure. Let my home be the place where Your character takes root, and Your peace reigns.

Part Two: The Inner Work of REFINEMENT

CHAPTER 5 - THE CRUCIBLE OF SELF IN COVENANT

For every heart learning to die to self so that love may live, may this fire lead you to deeper surrender and peace.

The Hidden Fire Within the Covenant

Every believer enters marriage with the desire to love and be loved, but few realize that the truest test of love is not between two people; it is within one's heart.

The crucible of self is the inner fire where pride, fear, and control are burned away. It is not your spouse who refines you first; it is the presence of God revealing you to you through them.

"... If anyone desires to come after Me, let him deny himself, and take up his cross daily, and follow Me."

Luke 9:23 (NKJV)

Marriage magnifies what singleness only hinted at; it exposes our hidden motives, the need to be right, the fear of being unseen. In those moments, the Holy Spirit whispers, "This is where you die to self, not to lose, but to live differently."

The War Between "Me" and "We"

There is a quiet battle that happens in every marriage: **the war between me and we.**

It shows up in small choices: who yields, who apologizes first, whose way becomes the final say.

When self leads, unity suffers, but when surrender leads, peace returns.

"Let nothing be done through selfish ambition or conceit, but in lowliness of mind let each esteem others better than himself."

Philippians 2:3

The covenant calls us to live for more than ourselves, so every time you choose peace over pride, you strengthen the "we" and every time you choose humility over argument, you protect your oneness.

The crucible of self teaches that love does not win by conquering the other, but by conquering self.

The Silent Distance: When Love Feels Far

There are moments in marriage when love still exists, yet closeness feels distant. When hands that once reached easily now hesitate and, in some cases, irritate.

When the warmth of togetherness cools quietly beneath the weight of unspoken hurts.

This distance is not always rebellion; sometimes, it is exhaustion. The body may rest beside another, but the heart stands guarded behind invisible walls. It is a silence that does not shout, yet it sighs.

In this space, many couples wonder: have we lost something sacred, or is God doing something deeper? The truth is that even intimacy can pass through the crucible. The nearness that once felt effortless becomes a place where patience and grace are refined.

"Two are better than one, because they have a good reward for their labor."

Ecclesiastes 4:9 (NKJV)

The crucible of self exposes pride not only in conflict but in closeness. When we expect affection on our terms, when we withdraw instead of communicating, when we let misunderstanding grow where mercy should have spoken. Love falters not because it fades, but because it forgets to listen.

Interestingly, the Spirit of God sometimes allows the warmth to wane so that we may learn again what true unity costs: time, tenderness, prayer, and humility. It is there, in the quiet ache between two hearts, that God begins to rebuild something stronger, affection anchored not in emotion, but in grace.

"And above all things have fervent love for one another, for 'love will cover a multitude of sins.'"

1 Peter 4:8

When words fail, and distance lingers, the gentle work of healing begins with one soft choice: to reach out again, to speak kindly again, to remember that love is not sustained by feeling but by faithfulness. God's presence can fill even the quiet spaces where passion once burned loud. He does not condemn the distance; He redeems it. And when two hearts surrender that silence back to Him, the warmth and intimacy that returns is not fleeting; **it is holy.**

The Death That Births Life

Self must die daily for the covenant to live continually.

Every act of surrender, every choice to listen, to yield, to forgive becomes a small resurrection.

"I have been crucified with Christ; it is no longer I who live, but Christ lives in me."

Galatians 2:20a

On my journey, I have found that the hardest apologies are often the most freeing. The times I wanted to be silent in pride were the moments God taught me that humility heals faster than explanations ever could. Dying to self does not erase your voice; it purifies it. It allows the Holy Spirit to speak peace through you, rather than you speaking from pain. And when self finally yields, life by the Spirit begins. The crucible does not ask us to try harder; it calls us to die deeper so that Christ may live through us.

"For if you live according to the flesh you will die; but if by the Spirit you put to death the deeds of the body, you will live."

Romans 8:13

The more we die to self, the more space Christ takes up in our marriages.

The Mirror of the Marriage Altar

Marriage is an altar where two living sacrifices meet daily, but one truth often shocks couples: God does not only use your spouse to refine you, He also uses you to refine your spouse. Does that make you feel better? That simply means your obedience to God becomes the tool that softens them, even when they resist. Your surrender becomes the soil where change begins to grow.

"... present your bodies a living sacrifice, holy, acceptable to God, which is your reasonable service."

Romans 12:1

If both husband and wife live this way: surrendering, serving, listening, love becomes unstoppable, but even when only one does, heaven still honors the heart that bows first because God measures obedience, not fairness. He moves through the one who stays soft in the fire.

In marriage, this death is not loss but exchange, our pride for His peace, our control for His counsel.

"For as many as are led by the Spirit of God, these are sons of God."

Romans 8:14 (NKJV)

The Danger of Self-Preservation

The greatest enemy of unity is self-preservation.

It whispers, "Protect yourself. Don't give too much. Don't be the one who always bends." And it feels justified at the moment, but when you guard yourself more than you guard love, the crucible stops working. The same fire that refines gold also hardens clay, but the difference lies in surrender.

"A new commandment I give to you, that you love one another; as I have loved you."

John 13:34a

Christ didn't preserve Himself; He poured Himself out, and that's what turns ordinary marriages into holy ones, when both hearts stop fighting to win and start fighting to serve. Love preserved becomes love alive. Self-preservation may feel like protection, but in marriage, it quietly blocks healing. It pushes a spouse to withdraw or defend instead of surrendering to God. Jesus gives the true path:

"... If anyone desires to come after Me, let him deny himself, and take up his cross daily, and follow Me."

Luke 9:23

Watchman Nee captured this clearly: "Without willingly and gladly accepting the principle of the cross, you cannot see the effect of the cross in your life; for its principle rests in denying self and trusting God." Self-preservation keeps the flesh in control; surrender invites Christ to lead.

"I have been crucified with Christ; it is no longer I who live, but Christ lives in me; and the life which I now live in the flesh I live by faith in the Son of God, who loved me and gave Himself for me."

Galatians 2:20

True transformation in marriage begins where self-preservation ends. Always know that self-preservation resists surrender, but the Cross requires it.

When Dying Feels Like Losing

There will be moments when dying to self feels like defeat, when you forgive first, apologize first, or stay patient while your spouse seems unmoved, but heaven sees what humility hides, and no surrender goes unnoticed by God.

"Humble yourselves in the sight of the Lord, and He will lift you up."

James 4:10

Let me remind you again that the Cross looked like loss until the third day. **Until the third day.** Your obedience may feel small now, but resurrection always follows surrender. The fire that humbles you today will honor you tomorrow, so keep yielding and keep trusting. The Refiner never forgets what the fire costs you.

When Both Choose the Cross

There is a beautiful turning point that happens when both hearts yield. The tension that once burned painfully begins to warm instead of wound. In many marriages, including some I have had the privilege to counsel, both are passionate believers, yet locked in a quiet war of pride.

Dr. David Yonggi Cho once shared how a couple in his church, on the brink of divorce, was restored in the place of prayer when he recognized that their battle was more than physical. It was spiritual, so he entered what he called "the fourth dimension," applying the Cross and the power of the Holy Spirit to the picture of their broken union. He visited their home, held their hands, and prayed with them. The wall of hatred and pride between the couple died a natural death, and they reconciled at once, apologizing to each other. When both choose the cross, walls fall faster than anyone can imagine. Love becomes worship again.

Remember that it is not about who surrenders first; that is what the flesh wants. Rather, it is about meeting at the altar together.

"Love suffers long and is kind; love does not envy; love does not parade itself, is not puffed up... endures all things."

1 Corinthians 13:4,7

The miracle of mutual surrender is that it does not just restore a marriage, it revives hearts.

Reflection Moment

"Where am I still protecting my pride instead of preserving peace? What parts of self need to surrender so that love can thrive?"

Lord, help me die to everything in me that competes with Your love. Teach me to yield when I want to win, to listen when I want to speak, and to serve even when I do not feel seen. Refine my heart until Christ is visible in the way I love. Father, teach me to be humble enough to change, patient enough to wait, and wise enough to let Your Spirit lead me. Let the crucible of self make me more like You."

CHAPTER 6 - THE WEIGHT OF WORDS AND THE WISDOM OF SILENCE

For every heart learning when to speak and when to be still, may your words build peace and your silence become prayer.

The Power That Shapes the Atmosphere

Words are never neutral because every sentence carries the power to shape the atmosphere of a home; to heal or to harm, to build or to break.

"Death and life are in the power of the tongue, and those who love it will eat its fruit."

Proverbs 18:21

In life and most importantly in marriage, words become seeds, meaning that what you sow repeatedly becomes what you live daily. So, be incredibly careful. E.W. Kenyon and Don Gossett write in *The Power of Your Words Devotional* that "some people pride themselves on their quick tempers and witty retorts, but God calls it a virtue to be slow to anger."

In the heat of marriage, this truth becomes a mirror for the soul. The fire that refines our speech also exposes the impatience within us, and every sharp word quenched by grace becomes a victory in the unseen battle of character.

"Do not hasten in your spirit to be angry, for anger rests in the bosom of fools."

Ecclesiastes 7:9

When love is spoken gently, peace grows, but when anger is spoken harshly, walls rise.

Sometimes even love can sound harsh when the heart is overwhelmed, but this should never become normal in marriage. On the other hand, anger doesn't always shout; sometimes it speaks softly through manipulation, sarcasm, or disguised resentment, so spouses must discern both tone and intention.

True love chooses gentleness because gentleness keeps the heart open. Scripture teaches that a soft answer turns away wrath. (Proverbs 15:1) Husbands and wives must learn the discipline of speaking the right words in the right season and letting gentleness lead the conversation.

God designed words to create life. He spoke the world into existence, so when we speak with His Spirit, our homes begin to sound like heaven.

When Words Wound

Anger has a sound, same for pride, impatience, and disappointment. They are all cousins who roll together with similar characteristics. The wrong word spoken at a vulnerable or sensitive moment can pierce deeper than silence ever could.

"A soft answer turns away wrath, but a harsh word stirs up anger."

Proverbs 15:1

Again, in some scenarios, the test is not what we say, but how we say it. Tone can betray what the heart hides, and even truth without tenderness can sound like rejection. God calls us to speak as those who carry His presence, aware that every word is heard twice: once by the listener and once by heaven. Silence, when ruled by the Spirit, is not repression; it is refinement. It is in stillness that wisdom gains its voice, and love regains its tone.

The Holy Work of Restraint

Silence is not weakness.

In the kingdom of God, silence can also be strength, a moment of choosing patience over reaction.

"... be swift to hear, slow to speak, slow to wrath."

James 1:19

There are moments when silence becomes worship, when instead of answering in frustration, you let the Holy Spirit intercede. In that pause, God often says more than your words ever could. Some of the greatest miracles in communication happen not through explanation, but through stillness.

The Spirit works best in the space humility leaves open.

Speaking with Grace and Truth

Grace without truth becomes flattery, and truth without grace becomes cruelty. But when the two meet in balance, in gentleness, in wisdom, the Word Himself is revealed through us.

> ***"Let your speech always be with grace, seasoned with salt, that you may know how you ought to answer each one."***
>
> ***Colossians 4:6***

To speak with grace is to allow God to filter your words before they leave your mouth. It means asking, "Is this word necessary? Is it kind? Does it bring peace?"

Words alone—cruel words—have destroyed many homes, so let us apply grace. Grace does not mean avoiding correction; it means delivering truth with the tone of love.

When Silence Speaks More Than Words

Silence can be an act of faith.

It says, "I trust God to defend me, to speak for me, to bring understanding in His time."

"The Lord will fight for you, and you shall hold your peace."

Exodus 14:14

There are moments when the Holy Spirit says, "Be still," and stillness is not the absence of thought, but the presence of wisdom. When the heart rests, clarity rises, and in that quiet, you begin to hear God again. You hear His correction, His comfort, His direction. And often, He reminds you that peace is a person, not a product of conversation.

The Language of the Spirit

When Christ fills a home, even ordinary speech carries heaven's tone, or we may call it rhythm.

The Holy Spirit teaches us to use our words as healing balm, not as weapons of defense.

"The mouth of the righteous is a well of life."

Proverbs 10:11a

The language of the Spirit is gentle, truthful, and timely. It does not rush to be heard, but it seeks first to understand. When both husband and wife learn to speak this way, **conversation becomes communion.**

Reflection Moment

"Have my word, built peace or broken it? Do I speak to be right or to bring reconciliation?"

Lord, teach me the weight of my words. Purify my tone until my speech sounds like grace. Give me wisdom to know when to speak and when to be still. Let every word from my mouth reflect Your heart.

CHAPTER 7 - HEALING IN THE FIRE: FORGIVENESS AND RESTORATION

For every wound still aching beneath the surface, may the fire that once burned you now become the warmth that heals you.

After the Breaking Comes the Mending

Every marriage will face moments when something cracks: a word too sharp, a silence too long, a wound too deep. But in God's hands, breaking is never the end; it is the beginning of healing. God is near to the fractured heart. He does not discard what is damaged, but He restores it with grace. Mending begins not when one says, "I'm sorry," but when both say, "Lord, make us whole again." Forgiveness does not erase the past, but it opens the door for peace to enter the present.

"...to give them beauty for ashes, the oil of joy for mourning."

Isaiah 61:3

The breaking reveals our need for mercy. The mending reveals God's ability to make even pain purposeful. And when the healing comes, it often looks quieter than expected. Not perfect, but peaceful. When self finally bows, the heart becomes soft enough for healing. Surrender opens the door that pride once locked. It is there, right there in that quiet space after the argument, when silence feels heavy, that God whispers, "Now, let Me mend it."

"He heals the brokenhearted and binds up their wounds."

Psalm 147:3 (NKJV)

Always remember that healing is not always dramatic; sometimes it begins with one prayer whispered through tears: "Lord, help me forgive them." And the moment you say it, even if your heart is not ready, heaven starts to move.

The Cost of Holding On

Unforgiveness feels like control, but it is a horrible cage that does not protect you. It poisons you.

"For if you forgive men their trespasses, your heavenly Father will also forgive you."

Matthew 6:14

I once counseled a woman who said, "I'll never forgive him, not after what he keeps doing."

These words and heart posture opened the door to the enemy to afflict her with an infirmity that God had already taken away years ago. A husband can change and grow softer, while the wife grows bitter. It can be vice versa, too. Unforgiveness is a deadly poison that can freeze you in the season of your hurt, but when you forgive, you release the event from repeating itself in your emotions.

You tell your soul, "I am free to move forward."

Let go and let God!

When Forgiveness Feels Impossible

Some wounds are deeper than disappointment, betrayal, or rejection. Words that left invisible scars.

You may feel, "If I forgive, they win." But forgiveness is not about victory. It is about freedom.

Your freedom.

"... Father, forgive them, for they do not know what they do."

Luke 23:34a

There was a time I prayed that prayer through clenched teeth, and I did not want to pray it because I did not feel forgiving. I felt broken, but the moment I obeyed God's Word, something in me lifted. Forgiveness did not change the memory, but it changed the meaning. When you forgive, you stop allowing the pain to define the narrative.

You let the Holy Spirit become the Author again.

The Slow Work of Restoration

Forgiveness is a moment; healing is a process.

Sometimes the feelings take time to follow the decision, but do not mistake your lingering sadness for failure. It is just your soul catching up with your obedience.

"He has made everything beautiful in its time."

Ecclesiastes 3:11a

I once met a woman who had not spoken kindly in months with the husband, spanning into years. Each conversation between them was guarded, every look defensive, and depression had set in. It deeply worried me because it reflected on the spiritual atmosphere of their home and, most importantly, the children. In cases like this, counseling, both spiritual and physical, is highly recommended to diagnose the root foundation of the problem and to create the opportunity for restoration. For another family, the remedy might be a brief note saying, "I'm still angry, but I miss our friendship/favorite meal." Such messages can communicate a willingness to forgive and trigger restoration. Restoration begins with one act of softness. God rebuilds what is broken brick by brick. And the person grows in honesty, patience, and daily grace.

Healing Becomes Testimony

Every scar tells a story, not of what was destroyed, but of what survived. God never wastes pain; He repurposes it.

"And we know that all things work together for good to those who love God."

Romans 8:28a

I have seen marriages that almost ended in divorce become ministries that healed others. Testimonies like, "We're not just together, we're restored."

That is what grace does; it turns graves into gardens.

Forgiveness might begin with tears, but it ends with testimony.

And when you finally see beauty rise from ashes, you will know the fire did not destroy you; it defined you.

Reflection Moment

"What hurt am I still holding onto that God wants to heal? What would happen if I released it fully to Him today?"

Lord, teach me to forgive like You. Heal the parts of me that still bleed when touched. Make me an instrument of Your restoration. Let my heart tell a story of grace that outlives my pain.

Part Three: The Outward Witness of REFINEMENT

CHAPTER 8 - HANDLING THE HEAT: ABUSE, BOUNDARIES, AND SAFETY

For every soul walking through the fire of harm or fear, may this truth set you free: God's love does not bruise. His covenant does not crush.

Truth Before Tradition

The sanctity of marriage must never silence the cry of the wounded. God hates divorce, yes, but He hates violence more.

The covenant was never designed to be a prison, and submission was never meant to be survival.

"For the Lord God of Israel says that He hates divorce, for it covers one's garment with violence."

Malachi 2:16

Where there is abuse, manipulation, or control, the Spirit of Christ grieves. Marriage reflects Christ and the Church, and Christ never abuses His bride. Safety is not rebellion, and boundaries are not disobedience. Let me say this: applying wisdom is not faithlessness.

The Line Between Refinement and Destruction

There is a difference between the crucible that refines and the fire that consumes. Refinement draws you closer to God, but destruction drives you into fear. God may use tension to grow patience, but He never uses terror to teach submission, so any relationship that crushes identity, isolates, or intimidates is breaking the law of love.

"There is no fear in love; but perfect love casts out fear, because fear involves torment."

1 John 4:18a

If your safety or sanity is at risk, the wisest thing you can do is step into the light.

Speak to someone safe and seek counsel, not condemnation.

The crucible of God burns pride and selfishness, not people.

Boundaries Are Biblical

Boundaries do not betray faith; they define stewardship. Even Jesus withdrew from crowds when danger arose. He did not call avoidance cowardice; He called it timing.

"Therefore they sought to take Him; but no one laid a hand on Him, because His hour had not yet come."

John 7:30

To set a boundary is to acknowledge that you are God's property: your life, your body, and your peace belong to Him.

Love is not a license for harm.

Many have gone to an early grave because they misunderstood that safety is a priority in marriage, especially when there is a threat to life. I once had a conversation with a woman who initially professed that death from abuse in marriage was a natural occurrence. She had believed and accepted this trauma as the way she would die until deliverance came. She learned to set boundaries that helped her escape death in her marriage. The same God who tells us to forgive also tells us to guard our hearts.

"Keep your heart with all diligence, for out of it spring the issues of life."

Proverbs 4:23

You can walk in forgiveness and still walk away from danger, and you can honor the covenant while choosing safety. Forgiveness reconciles the soul, but wisdom protects the body.

Separation, Not Abandonment

There are seasons when stepping aside becomes an act of faith, not failure.

Temporary separation, under prayer and counsel, may be the space God uses for repentance, accountability, or healing. It does not dissolve love; it defines it. It says, "I will not help you sin against yourself or me." The separation allows God to work without the constant cycle of harm.

"The prudent see danger and take refuge."

Proverbs 22:3a (NIV)

Heaven's desire is not endurance without safety but restoration through truth.

A marriage healed by honesty is stronger than one held together by silence.

The Ministry of Healing

Abuse leaves more than bruises; it leaves belief wounds. "I deserved it." "God is punishing me."

"I cannot speak because people will not believe me..." These sentences are not from God.

Jesus says, **"Come to Me, and I will give you rest."**

"The Spirit of the Lord is upon Me, because He has anointed Me to preach the gospel to the poor; He has sent Me to heal the brokenhearted, to proclaim liberty to the captives."

Luke 4:18a

Healing from abuse is a process, but it begins the moment we speak the truth. Grace does not erase accountability; it empowers recovery. God restores dignity first, then direction.

If this is your situation, hear me: you are not what happened to you. You are who God calls you.

And He still calls you, His beloved.

For the Church and the Helper

To every pastor, friend, or intercessor who hears the cry of the wounded, please believe them and protect them. Pray with discernment but act with compassion.

Silence in the face of suffering is not neutrality; it is agreement with injustice.

The Church plays a vital role in supporting marriages, especially when conflicts arise, so it must become a safe crucible, a place of truth and tenderness, not shame. In addressing issues between couples, leaders must avoid being one-sided. Every story has two sides, and both deserve to be heard with patience and understanding. True wisdom is found not in taking sides but in guiding both parties toward truth, healing, and restoration. While prayer and spiritual counsel remain essential, we must encourage couples to seek help from qualified Christian counselors who can offer professional guidance rooted in biblical values.

When the Church combines spiritual insight with professional support, it strengthens the home, upholds justice, and becomes a true channel of grace and reconciliation.

"Open your mouth for the speechless, in the cause of all who are appointed to die."

Proverbs 31:8

Where grace and justice meet, God's glory dwells.

Reflection Moment

"Lord, where do I need Your healing in my heart, my marriage, or my boundaries? Have I mistaken endurance for holiness?? Have I allowed fear or silence to replace truth and wisdom?"

Father, heal every place where love has been distorted by pain. Give me courage to seek help, wisdom to walk in truth, and grace to forgive without surrendering safety. Teach me that safety is not sin, and that peace is still possible after pain. Make me a voice of truth and a vessel of healing to others. Restore what has been broken, in Your way, in Your time.

CHAPTER 9 - INTERFERENCES: IN-LAWS, FRIENDS, AND OUTSIDE VOICES

For every home surrounded by voices, may God teach you to hear love without losing peace, and to honor others without losing unity.

When God joined Adam and Eve, He didn't just create the first marriage;

He also set the first boundary.
He said,

"Therefore a man shall leave his father and mother and be joined to his wife, and they shall become one flesh." (Genesis 2:24)

That verse isn't about rejection; it's about realignment.

When Too Many Voices Speak

While some voices bless, others burden. The ability to tell the difference is part of spiritual maturity.

Every marriage begins with two people, but rarely stays that way. Parents, siblings, friends, mentors, and even well-meaning believers often bring advice, expectations, and opinions that can shape how a couple lives and loves. Influence is not the problem; interference is. God designed marriage to include community, but not to be controlled by it.

"Therefore a man shall leave his father and mother and be joined to his wife, and they shall become one flesh."

Genesis 2:24

Leaving does not mean dishonor; it means reordering loyalties. The voice of the husband becomes the first human voice of priority after God in every home. Any voice that competes with that order, even in love, weakens the oneness God designed.

The Blessing and the Boundary of Family

In-laws can be a blessing when they choose to support, not supervise, but even godly families can cross into control when they forget that counsel is not command. Family is a gift from God, but blessings need boundaries, and love without wisdom can become interference. Newly married couples should be left alone to separate from families so they can nurture their young and tender marriage right from the beginning and build their home without interference. This separation is not rebellion but the divine order of "leaving and cleaving," which allows a new covenant to take root and grow strong before outside voices are invited in. When we honour boundaries, peace remains, and family ties stay healthy.

"Honor your father and your mother."

Exodus 20:12a

"Therefore a man shall leave..."

Genesis 2:24a

Scripture holds both truths together: honor and leave. To honor without leaving leads to dependency, and to leave without honor leads to rebellion. The key is balance, which is gratitude for the past, boundaries for the present, and agreement for the future. Parents should be respected, not revered as rulers over a new home. Couples must learn to guard their unity from well-intentioned intrusions.

Protecting Your Covenant, Not Your Image

I once counselled a couple who unintentionally kept weakening their marriage by running to their families every time conflict arose. When frustrated, they shared personal stories in a way that made the other look worse than they really were. Before long, relatives took sides and spoke disrespectfully about the spouse, not because the marriage was broken, but because the couple repeatedly opened the door for outsiders to judge what should have remained within the covenant.

Scripture tells us,

"And above all things have fervent love for one another, 'for love will cover a multitude of sins.'"

1 Peter 4:8.

Love protects dignity, and it does not expose weakness for sympathy. Couples must intentionally cover each other with honor.

"A soft answer turns away wrath."

Proverbs 15:1a

Sometimes, that soft answer is the choice to speak carefully about your spouse when emotions are high. Never make your partner look small to appear innocent, and never exaggerate a story to gain support. The moment you misrepresent your spouse to outsiders, you give others permission to misjudge, dishonor, and interfere with the covenant God entrusted only to the two of you.

Friends: Counsel or Confusion?

Friends can either stabilize or sabotage a marriage. The difference lies in whether they lead you toward your spouse or away from them.

"Do not be deceived: 'Evil company corrupts good habits.'"

1 Corinthians 15:33

A friend who always sides with your pain will eventually become a wall between you and reconciliation, but a friend who reminds you of your covenant becomes a bridge back to peace. Be careful whose voice you invite into your frustration because some people pour oil; others pour gasoline. Which one do you desire?

The wrong confidant can turn temporary conflict into lasting distance, so the wisest couples learn to share with God first, then with a trusted spiritual guide, **not with the crowd.**

The Role of the Church Community

The Church is called to strengthen marriages, not to compare or control them. Fellowship is healthy when it restores, not when it performs. Every couple needs a faith community, one rooted in grace, not gossip.

"Bear one another's burdens, and so fulfill the law of Christ."

Galatians 6:2

Accountability in love brings growth, but exposure in judgment brings shame. Leaders and believers alike must remember that not all marital struggles are invitations for intervention. Some require prayer more than presence, and intercession more than investigation. Let's make it a priority to guard another couple's privacy because it is as holy as guarding your own purity.

Recognizing Manipulation and Emotional Control

Sometimes interference doesn't look harmful. It can come wrapped in guilt, flattery, or "concern,"

but the fruit reveals the root.

If a person consistently undermines peace, questions loyalty, or fosters suspicion, they are not being led by the Spirit of Christ.

"For where envy and self-seeking exist, confusion and every evil thing are there."

James 3:16

Discernment is love's armor. This is not about suspicion, but about spiritual clarity. Ask yourself, **"Does this voice bring peace or pressure? Unity or unrest?"** When you discern manipulation, confront it with grace, not hostility.

You can love people without letting them lead you.

When God Uses Outside Voices for Good

Not all outside voices are negative.

Sometimes God sends wise mentors, counselors, and intercessors who help rekindle understanding and guide reconciliation.

"Where there is no counsel, the people fall; but in the multitude of counselors there is safety."

Proverbs 11:14

The key is spiritual maturity. A godly mentor never replaces the Holy Spirit; they help you hear Him more clearly. They build, not break, and they guide, not govern. When counsel aligns with Scripture and confirms peace, it often carries the voice of God.

Guarding the Gate Together

Every marriage must learn to guard its gate, to decide, together, which voices are welcome.

This is not control; it is stewardship. The gate of your home must be closed to confusion and open to counsel that carries Christ's fragrance.

"... My well-beloved has a vineyard on a very fruitful hill. He dug it up and cleared out its stones, and planted it with the choicest vine."

Isaiah 5:1-2

What God plants must be protected. Couples who pray together about whose advice to follow find strength in unity and clarity in decision-making.

The moment two agree before God, outside noises lose their power.

Reflection Moment

"Which voices have I allowed too much access to my heart and home? Do my conversations about my spouse invite peace or deepen division?"

Lord, teach us to honor others without losing our oneness. Give us wisdom to discern who speaks with Your heart. Surround our marriage with voices that build, not break, and let our agreement silence every other sound.

CHAPTER 10 - MARRIAGE AS MINISTRY

Every marriage has a message.

Some tell a story of endurance. Some tell a story of forgiveness. And some tell a story of healing after loss. All are meant to tell a story of grace that endures.

For every couple learning to serve beyond themselves, may your love become a testimony, your home a sanctuary, and your union a message that reveals Jesus.

The Divine Blueprint

Marriage is not man's invention; it is heaven's design.

It was never meant to be just a social arrangement, but a sacred assignment.

"For this reason a man shall leave his father and mother and be joined to his wife, and the two shall become one flesh."

Ephesians 5:31

When God created marriage, He created a living parable of Christ and the Church, which is a daily reflection of divine love played out in human hearts. Every act of kindness, patience, and forgiveness between husband and wife preaches the gospel without words. Your union is not just about happiness; it is about holiness. Marriage was created to be the first ministry on earth, the foundation of every other assignment.

Before the Church, there was the couple. Before the pulpit, there was the home.

"Therefore what God has joined together, let not man separate."

Mark 10:9

God's order has never changed: Christ is the head of man, man is the head of his wife, and they both are submitted to the Spirit of God. This is not a hierarchy of worth but a structure of responsibility. When each person understands their divine position, peace flows. Once the husband loves as Christ loves, submission is not a struggle. When the wife honors as the Church honors, leadership is not a burden. Once the order is broken, and pride replaces purpose or control replaces care, the marriage begins to mirror the confusion of the world rather than the harmony of heaven. The divine blueprint of marriage is not about who leads louder, but who loves deeper. The true mark of authority is humility, which requires revelation, light, and obedience.

"Submitting to one another in the fear of God."

Ephesians 5:21

The design of marriage is never discovered by emotion or tradition; it is revealed by divine illumination. As Apostle Arome Osayi writes in

Choices, "Only a will illuminated by God can make the right choices. A proof of growth in our relationship with God is that we easily discern and set out to execute His will."

His will is His divine blueprint for marriage. When the will is submitted to God and the mind renewed by His Word, the choices we make within marriage become expressions of obedience.

> ***"Every good gift and every perfect gift is from above, and comes down from the Father of lights, with whom there is no variation or shadow of turning."***
>
> ***James 1:17***

Marriage, then, becomes a living altar where two wills continually yield to divine direction. Only when the light of God governs both hearts can His blueprint be truly built upon. Every home that carries peace carries the presence of God, and every couple that chooses grace over pride becomes a ministry in motion.

Choose wisely.

The Marriage Altar

Marriage begins at an altar; it is not a stage.

It is not a performance for people to watch but a covenant for God to witness. When you stood before Him and said, "I do," you entered ministry. From that moment, your first congregation became your spouse, and your first mission field became your home. Yes, the first mission field is the home.

"And whatever you do, do it heartily, as to the Lord and not to men."

Colossians 3:23

When love grows weary, remember: the altar where you began is still open. Every time you pray together, forgive each other, or serve one another quietly, you are ministering to God Himself. Ministry is not only a pulpit and a microphone, but it is also the way you respond when no one claps.

The Divine Order

For a marriage to thrive in ministry, divine order must guide it. God is not the author of confusion, and His authority always flows through love, not control.

"But I want you to know that the head of every man is Christ, the head of woman is man, and the head of Christ is God."

1 Corinthians 11:3

Headship is not dominance; it is service, and submission is not silence; it is surrendered strength. When both husband and wife align under Christ's headship, harmony follows. The home becomes a sanctuary not of superiority, but of shared stewardship. Order invites anointing, but disorder invites exhaustion. When Christ is at the center, every role becomes worship, not warfare.

The Strength of the Praying Husband

A praying husband is the Priest of his home; he is the man who kneels before God before he stands before his family. His authority is not in his voice but in his surrender, so when he prays, heaven takes notice. His petitions carry weight not because of title or strength, but because of his covenant position. A husband's prayers form a hedge around his wife and children, becoming a spiritual covering that keeps the storms from breaking through.

Are you standing in the gap for your family as the priest of your home? Prayer turns leadership into stewardship, and it softens pride, corrects impatience, and teaches him to lead with tenderness. Keep in mind that the man who intercedes learns that true headship is not control but responsibility. It is not dominance, but divine accountability. The praying husband becomes the mirror of Christ in his home. Like Jesus, he lays down his desires to take up his cross in service. His altar becomes the furnace where decisions are purified, and his tears become seeds of preservation for his household. When the priest of the home prays, he opens gates for God's presence to dwell in the home. His prayer doesn't just protect, it transforms, aligning his heart with what heaven is saying. It is in that secret communion that he receives wisdom to lead, patience to love, and grace to endure the crucible with faith.

"Husbands, likewise, dwell with them with understanding, giving honor to the wife, as to the weaker vessel, and as being heirs together of the grace of life, that your prayers may not be hindered."

1 Peter 3:7

A husband who guards his prayer life guards the destiny of his family because, in his quiet strength, his wife finds confidence, and his children find safety. His prayer life becomes the anchor that steadies the family ship through the waves of the crucible.

The Strength of the Praying Wife

For every wife who feels unseen, unheard, or spiritually mismatched, heaven sees your labor of love. The crucible has a way of revealing not only your husband's weaknesses, but your own strength in *God.*

"The wise woman builds her house, but the foolish pulls it down with her hands."

Proverbs 14:1

It takes wisdom to know when to speak and when to pray. It takes grace to support a man without surrendering your identity, and it takes maturity to love him where he is, not where you wish he'd be. Some wives compare their husbands to men who seem more spiritual, more expressive, or more devoted to ministry, but comparison is a thief. It drains gratitude and blinds you to the quiet ways your husband already reflects God's grace. If your husband is not where you want him to be spiritually, remember: your prayers reach places your words never can. A gentle intercession can soften what criticism will only harden.

"The effective, fervent prayer of a righteous man avails much."

James 5:16b

God doesn't call wives to remake their husbands; He calls them to release them into His hands. He alone transforms hearts, so your assignment is not to manage him but to minister to him in love, in patience, and in consistent faith. A praying wife becomes a prophetic voice in her home not because she demands, but because she discerns. Her intercession shifts atmospheres, her tenderness breaks walls, her words invite the Holy Spirit where silence once reigned. There is nothing weak about a woman who would rather pray than complain. It is strength dressed in stillness, and with time, even the hardest heart learns to trust in God. So pray not that he would change to fit your measure of spirituality, but that he would encounter the God who already measures him with mercy. Again, you are not called to compete with his pace; you are called to complete his process.

"Who can find a virtuous wife? For her worth is far above rubies... Her husband also, and he praises her."

Proverbs 31:10, 28

Your prayer may not always be seen, but it is never wasted. Every whispered intercession becomes oil for your lamp, and one day, the same man who once struggled to lead will rise and thank God for the wife who refused to give up praying. You are the quiet fire in the home unseen by many, yet felt by all. Your strength is not in words but in intercession, not in striving but in surrender.

In prayer, you build unseen walls of protection around your husband and children. Your petitions soften what pride hardens and invite God's presence into the ordinary rhythm of family life. Prayer makes you a helper in the Spirit. You stand as a watchman and nurturer, carrying your husband's weaknesses to God instead of using them as weapons. Through your prayers, your home becomes a sanctuary of grace. A praying wife does not just maintain her home; she governs its atmosphere. Her words, seasoned by prayer, carry healing, and her faith steadies the entire household through every crucible.

When Leadership Limits Grace

There are few things more painful in a marriage than when leadership forgets love. When the man who was called to cover begins to control, when the one anointed to guide begins to silence. Many husbands mean well. They long to be respected, to lead well, to protect what is theirs, but when fear, pride, or insecurity shape that leadership, the result is not order but oppression. In the crucible of marriage, God tests the wife's submission and the husband's stewardship.

"Husbands, love your wives, just as Christ also loved the church and gave Himself for her."

Ephesians 5:25 (NKJV)

Christ's leadership was not about dominance; it was about dying. He didn't crush the Church's purpose; He empowered it. He didn't silence her voice; He sanctified it. Christ did not demand loyalty; He showed love. When a husband suppresses his wife's gifts or diminishes her calling because it threatens his own image, he is not leading like Christ; he is leading from fear and pride. The home becomes a prison, not a partnership. Every woman carries a grace; sometimes in prayer, sometimes in creativity, sometimes in ministry, sometimes in wisdom or compassion. When that grace is discouraged, something in the marriage dims.

"Husbands, likewise, dwell with them with understanding, giving honor to the wife, as to the weaker vessel, and as being heirs together of the grace of life."

1 Peter 3:7a

Leadership in love means lifting, not limiting. It means recognizing that your wife's strength is not competition, but completion. A wife's gifts are never a threat to her husband's calling, but they are tools for destiny. The true measure of godly leadership is not how many people follow, but how many flourish because of a husband's covering.

When a man leads in fear, his home becomes weary, but when he leads in love, his home becomes fruitful. A wise husband will ask, "Am I nurturing what God planted in her, or am I burying it? Heaven's order is never about one light outshining another. It is about two lights burning brighter together.

Serving Together

Every couple is called to serve, not necessarily on the same assignment, but with the same heart.

Some serve in pulpit ministry, others in parenting, others in business or compassion, and when both husband and wife understand that marriage itself is a ministry, their home becomes an altar of worship. Every meal shared, every disagreement resolved, every decision made together becomes a sacred act of service.

But all ministry begins in unity.

"Two are better than one, because they have a good reward for their labor."

Ecclesiastes 4:9

A divided marriage cannot multiply spiritually. When both hearts yield to one mission to reveal Christ, the ordinary becomes divine. Serving together strengthens intimacy, and it teaches teamwork. It deepens empathy and keeps the marriage outward-focused instead of inwardly offended.

Marriage ministry doesn't always require microphones or stages; sometimes, it is simply faithfulness behind closed doors. When the husband leads with love, and the wife supports with prayer, the anointing multiplies. Serving together does not mean doing the same thing; it means doing different things with the same heart. Unity is not uniformity; it is harmony. When you serve side by side, you discover that love and ministry share the same foundation: a foundation of sacrifice. Truly, the world doesn't need perfect marriages; it needs surrendered ones. Homes that model mercy and couples that embody Christ's compassion.

Love that carries light.

When the marriage itself becomes a sermon, no words are needed. The lantern simply burns, and others find their way by its glow.

Revealing Jesus Through Covenant

The ultimate purpose of marriage is not personal fulfillment, but divine reflection. Your marriage is a mirror where the world should see Jesus, His mercy, His faithfulness, His forgiveness.

"By this all will know that you are My disciples, if you have love for one another."

John 13:35

When others see how you handle conflict, extend grace, and stay committed through fire, they encounter a living sermon. The home becomes a testimony, not of perfection, but of redemption.

Every time you choose love, you preach Christ.

Every time you forgive, you preach resurrection.

Every time you reconcile, you preach grace.

A godly marriage glorifies the Creator, not the couple. The highest purpose of marriage is not companionship, comfort, or even personal growth; it is revelation. God designed marriage to be a living picture of His relationship with His Church, a visible demonstration of invisible grace. When a husband loves his wife sacrificially, and a wife honors her husband faithfully, something eternal is being revealed: the image of Christ and His bride.

Ephesians 5:31-32 says,

"For this reason a man shall leave his father and mother and be joined to his wife, and the two shall become one flesh.
This is a great mystery, but I speak concerning Christ and the church."

This "great mystery" is not about romance; it is about revelation. About God using ordinary human love to display extraordinary divine truth. When we forgive each other, we reveal His mercy. When we remain faithful through trials, we reveal His steadfastness. When we serve each other in humility, we reveal His servant heart. And when we choose reconciliation over revenge, we reveal His cross.

The goal is not a perfect marriage, but a Christ-shaped one.

And in that shaping, in the daily dying to self, in the stretching, in the surrender, the world begins to see Jesus. That is why the crucible is sacred, because it burns away pride so His humility can be seen. It melts down self-will so His love can flow. It breaks what hides Him so His glory can shine. Every time a couple allows the Holy Spirit to refine them, heaven rejoices because God is being glorified through their union. Their love becomes more than emotion; it becomes revelation.

2 Corinthians 4:6-7 reminds us,

"For it is the God who commanded light to shine out of darkness, who has shone in our hearts to give the light of the knowledge of the glory of God in the face of Jesus Christ.
But we have this treasure in earthen vessels, that the excellence of the power may be of God and not of us."

That's what marriage truly is: two earthen vessels carrying divine treasure. The cracks, the flaws, and the refining only make the treasure shine brighter. When others see patience instead of pride, peace instead of panic, and grace instead of grudges, they are not seeing us; they are seeing Him. This is the purpose of every Christian marriage: to make Jesus visible and to give God the glory. So that when people look at your life, they don't say, *"What a strong couple,"* but, *"What a faithful God."* In the end, marriage is not about man's success, but about God's glory. As Kenneth E. Hagin writes in his book *Love: The Way to Victory*, "When Jesus fulfilled the old covenant, He established a new covenant in His Blood."

"But now He has obtained a more excellent ministry, inasmuch as He is also Mediator of a better covenant, which was established on better promises."

Hebrews 8:6

The blood of Jesus is a covenant of love for His bride to reveal His glory. Let your home be that revelation, not perfect, but pure; not proud, but peaceful; not loud with opinion, but filled with presence. When the world looks at your union, may they see the light of Christ burning steadily, even in the crucible.

The Weight of Responsibility

Marriage as ministry is not glamorous; it is sacred labor.

It requires prayer, boundaries, humility, and continual surrender. You are not just building a home; you are hosting the Holy Spirit.

"Unless the Lord builds the house, they labor in vain who build it."

Psalm 127:1a

Heaven watches how you love. Your children learn who God is by watching how you speak, how you forgive, how you lead, and how you follow. When marriage loses its ministry mindset, it becomes maintenance, but when ministry leads, joy returns, because you are no longer just living with each other, but for Him together.

The Reward of Covenant Faithfulness

Every couple that remains faithful through refinement carries a fragrance of heaven. Their story becomes an altar others can approach for hope.

"But may the God of all grace, who called us to His eternal glory by Christ Jesus, after you have suffered a while, perfect, establish, strengthen, and settle you."

1 Peter 5:10

The refining fire produces ministry that is pure. Not performance, but power through surrender. God doesn't just bless marriages that last; He blesses marriages that love well. Your endurance is not wasted; it is evangelism. Your unity is your witness. Your peace is your preaching.

The Legacy of Our Refining: What Our Children Learn from Our Fire

Every marriage carries more than two destinies; it carries generations.

What happens between a husband and wife never stays contained; it flows like a river through the lives of their children. Their silence speaks, and their tension teaches. When parents live in unity, children grow up under the covering of peace, but when pride, bitterness, or unhealed pain take root, it creates a fracture that doesn't stop at the couple. It ripples through the atmosphere of the home.

That is why the crucible matters. When we refuse to let God refine us, the heat doesn't go away; it passes on. Our children carry battles that were never meant for them. They question love, authority, and even God, not because they are rebellious, but because they are confused. Home is meant to be a sanctuary, but when it becomes a battlefield, young hearts grow up sad and weary before their time.

Proverbs 14:1 reminds us,

"The wise woman builds her house, but the foolish pulls it down with her hands."

Building or breaking a home begins with the spirit that governs it. When bitterness rules, peace leaves; when strife becomes normal, joy disappears; and where peace is absent, spiritual doors open that were meant to stay closed.

Ephesians 4:26-27 warns,

"'Be angry, and do not sin': do not let the sun go down on your wrath, nor give place to the devil."

Every unhealed argument, every unrepentant wound, every unresolved grudge becomes an open door, and the enemy does not waste open doors. He walks through them.

Jesus said in ***Matthew 12:25,***

"... 'Every kingdom divided against itself is brought to desolation, and every city or house divided against itself will not stand.'"

Children are often the most sensitive to these unseen battles. They feel the tension even when words aren't spoken. They carry anxiety they cannot name, and in their search for peace, they may reach for comfort in the wrong places—friends, habits, or influences that promise relief but lead to destruction and sometimes death. When the spiritual covering of peace is broken, children become vulnerable to emotional confusion, fear, and even the enemy's schemes. Not because God withdraws, but because the protective walls are cracked. But there is good news: what has been opened by strife can be closed by repentance. When parents humble themselves before God, even privately, even after years, heaven responds. The same grace that restores a marriage also restores the home's covering. Forgiveness mends not just hearts but spiritual boundaries. Peace returns like a strong wind closing every open gate.

2 Chronicles 7:14 promises,

"If My people who are called by My name will humble themselves, and pray and seek My face, and turn from their wicked ways, then I will hear from heaven, and will forgive their sin and heal their land."

That "land" includes your home. Your living room. Your children's hearts. When grace reignites love between husband and wife, it doesn't just heal them; it teaches their children what redemption looks like. It shows that broken things can be rebuilt. It teaches the next generation that love is not perfect, but it is powerful when God is at the center. Even if your children have witnessed tension or pain, it is never too late to show them peace. It is never too late to rebuild the altar of prayer in your home. It is never too late to shut every door the enemy once used to sow fear. Your home can burn again with holy fire, not of anger, but of grace, and your children will grow up remembering not the fights that happened, but the faith that followed, because the truest legacy you can leave them is not wealth or comfort -

it is a healed home that reflects God's love.

Psalm 112:1-2 says,

***"Blessed is the man who fears the Lord, who delights greatly in His commandments.
His descendants will be mighty on earth; the generation of the upright will be blessed."***

That is the power of a refined marriage. It secures the future of the next generation, and it cuts off the enemy's access. It releases blessings and peace like an inheritance. Let your children see that grace is stronger than pride, that prayer is louder than anger, and that love refined in God's fire cannot be destroyed. When your marriage bows to the crucible, your children rise in freedom.

Reflection Moment

"Does my marriage reveal Christ's leadership and the Church's love? Have I used authority to control or prayer to restore? Do we serve together, or do we compete silently?"

Lord, use our marriage as a light for others. Let the way we love each other draw hearts to You. Teach us to see our home as holy ground, a place where Your presence dwells and Your grace flows freely. Heal every wound in our children that came from our brokenness. Close every door the enemy has used, and fill our home with Your peace.

Part Four: The Broader Fires of FAITH

CHAPTER 11 - BALANCING THE ALTAR AND THE HOME

Every calling has a cost, but marriage should never be the price.

In every generation, God raises men and women with powerful anointing, pastors, prophets, worshippers, intercessors, and evangelists. But many lose sight of a simple truth: before God called you *to the altar of ministry,* He entrusted you *with the altar of your home.* Ministry and marriage are not enemies ...They were both created by God, and both should reflect His glory. But if we do not balance them out, one can drain the other.

The Divine Order of Priority

God → Marriage → Ministry → Everything else.

That is the order of heaven's design.

1 Timothy 3:4-5 (NIV) gives a sobering reminder:

"He must manage his own family well and see that his children obey him, and he must do so in a manner worthy of full respect.
(If anyone does not know how to manage his own family, how can he take care of God's church?)."

Our first discipleship begins at home. If the home is neglected, the ministry loses credibility, and if the marriage collapses, the message weakens, not because God fails, but because the vessel grows weary.

Your spouse is not your distraction from ministry; they are your *first ministry.* The covenant you nurture together becomes the soil that sustains every other calling. When the soil is healthy, ministry bears fruit, but when the soil is dry, ministry becomes performance.

When Ministry Takes Too Much

Even good work can become an idol when it consumes what God meant to stay sacred. If your schedule never leaves room for connection, if prayer at home becomes rare while public prayer increases, if your spouse or children are silently enduring loneliness while you pour out to others, it is time to pause. **Jesus Himself modeled balance.**

After ministering to the crowds, He often withdrew with His disciples to rest and pray ***(Mark 6:31).***

He never sacrificed a relationship for results.

You can serve people and still protect peace. You can love God deeply and still set boundaries. Grace does not excuse exhaustion; it empowers order.

Not Competing

In healthy marriages, both partners find their rhythm in ministry, not always doing the same thing, but moving in the same Spirit. One may preach, another intercede. One may lead publicly while the other builds quietly, but both roles carry equal weight before God.

Ecclesiastes 4:9-10 reminds us:

"Two are better than one, because they have a good reward for their labor.
For if they fall, one will lift up his companion."

Partnership does not mean identical calling. It means united purpose, and when couples support each other's assignments without competition, grace multiplies. When they compare or compete, grace diminishes. The key is humility and recognizing that both altars, public and private, belong to the same King.

The Home as the First Altar

Every home is an altar, whether we tend it or not.

Genesis 2:15 says,

"Then the Lord God took the man and put him in the garden of Eden to tend and keep it."

That garden represents the first assignment: the home. God didn't call Adam to preach first; He called him to *cultivate and guard*. In the same way, your marriage and family are your first field of ministry. The home is where you prove that your anointing is genuine; not in crowds, but in consistency; not in sermons, but in service; not in applause, but in attitude. When the home becomes a place of prayer, the ministry gains power.

When the home becomes neglected, the ministry loses oil.

Finishing Well

Many start strong in ministry but finish alone. They gave God their platform but lost their partner, and that is not God's desire. He doesn't just want you to *serve well;* God wants you to *end well.* Ending well means coming to the end of your assignment with your faith intact, your love alive, and your family still standing beside you.

That's why protecting balance isn't selfish; it is sacred stewardship.

Let your ministry and marriage fuel each other, not fight each other. Let your public fire be sustained by your private devotion. Let your spouse feel honored, not overshadowed, by your calling. When people look at your life, may they see both a fruitful ministry *and* a flourishing marriage: a balance that brings glory to God. When the altar and the home walk in harmony, heaven rejoices.

Keeping Heaven in View

In the end, every calling, whether in marriage, ministry, or both, leads to one ultimate goal: ***to make heaven.***

It is possible to be busy for God and still drift from Him. It is possible to build a public ministry and lose a private walk, but it is not God's will that we labor here and miss eternity.

Matthew 16:26a asks,

"For what profit is it to a man if he gains the whole world, and loses his own soul?"

Heaven is not a distant dream; it is the destination of every refined believer, and how we love, serve, forgive, and endure both in marriage and in ministry determines whether we walk that narrow path. When your heart stays humble, your home stays holy. When your motives stay pure, your ministry stays fruitful. When both stay surrendered, your eternity stays secure.

Never forget: We are not just building ministries; we are building eternal testimonies. *The goal is not recognition, but redemption.* Not applause, but arrival, *to stand before Him unashamed.*

So, let your marriage and ministry point heavenward. Let every act of love, every moment of obedience, every tear of repentance become a step closer to that eternal reward.

Reflection Moment

"What fire have we come through, and what flame must we now carry? Whose life can our story ignite with hope?"

Lord, thank You for the refining, for the fire that did not consume but completed us. May our love be the lantern that points others back to You. Let every word we speak, every act we share, and every promise we keep shine with the light of Your grace. In our home, in our hearts, and in our generation, **let there be light.**

CHAPTER 12 - THE LEGACY OF THE LIGHT

The crucible was never meant to end with pain. It was meant to end with purpose. Every flame that survives the refining carries a testimony that cannot be hidden.

From Fire to Flame

When the disciples walked with Jesus, they didn't understand that the fire He carried would one day rest upon them. They watched Him suffer, they saw Him rise, and then they were filled, not with fear, but with fire. In much the same way, marriage becomes a place where the fire that once tested you becomes the fire that fuels you. What once burned in secret now shines with purpose.

The same love that was purified in the crucible now burns as a light for others.

"Then there appeared to them divided tongues, as of fire, and one sat upon each of them."

Acts 2:3

Refined couples become ministers of flame. They carry peace where others carry pain, patience where others carry pride, and forgiveness where others carry fear.

They become walking testimonies that the Covenant still works because Christ still reigns.

The Marriage That Ministers Without Words

There is a quiet kind of evangelism that doesn't come from preaching, but from living.

When a husband and wife walk in grace, their union preaches the gospel more powerfully than a thousand sermons.

"By this all will know that you are My disciples, if you have love for one another."

John 13:35

Love becomes the language of the Spirit. Unity becomes the sermon of faith. Patience becomes the altar of surrender. Every argument resolved in prayer becomes a message of mercy. Every wound healed in humility becomes a testimony of grace.

Your marriage was not meant to just survive the fire; it was meant to shine because of it.

The flame that refined you now draws others to the warmth of God's love.

Guarding the Flame

Every light must be tended, and a lantern left untended will dim, not because it lacks oil, but because it is neglected. So, guard the flame.

Pray together. Forgive quickly. Laugh often. Rest without guilt. Keep Christ at the center.

"Do not quench the Spirit."

1 Thessalonians 5:19

The world will always try to pull you away from your altar, but if you guard your time in God and your love for one another, no storm will ever fully put out your flame. Guarding the flame is not about perfection; it is about protection. You protect what you have endured to build.

You defend what God has entrusted you with.

The Legacy of the Light

Every crucible births a legacy, and every legacy begins with obedience. The way you love your spouse teaches your children how to love. The way you forgive teaches them what grace looks like.

And the way you endure teaches them that the covenant is sacred, not seasonal.

The light you carry will outlive you.

It will burn through the generations, through your home, your ministry, your children, and those who quietly watch your life from afar.

"Those who are wise shall shine like the brightness of the firmament, and those who turn many to righteousness like the stars forever and ever."

Daniel 12:3

The crucible was never just about you; it was about the God who refines through you.

Now that you have walked through the fire, He sends you back into the world as a living lantern, glowing with faith, wisdom, and the fragrance of His grace.

Now, you are not the same couple who began this journey. You are brighter. You are deeper. You are witnesses. Carry the flame. Light up homes with your forgiveness and hearts with your faith.

Light up the nations with your testimony. I am lighting mine too, and when others ask how your light survived the heat, simply smile and say,

"The God who refines is the same God who restores."

The Great Commission of the Covenant

"As the Father has sent Me, I also send you."

John 20:21b

When the refining is complete, the couple does not stay at the altar; they rise and go.

Every healed marriage becomes a voice. Every restored home becomes a testimony of redemption.

The world learns what grace looks like not from perfect couples, but from refined ones.

Marriage, at its purest, is a mission.

The same way Christ sent His disciples into the world, He sends couples into families, communities, and nations as living witnesses of His love. You are not just covenant partners -you are carriers of divine purpose. Live out the gospel in your union.

Let your forgiveness preach louder than offense. Let your joy outshine your trials. Let your unity testify of heaven.

And as your light shines, others will find their way back to the Source of every flame, the God who refines and restores.

A Final Benediction

"Now to Him who is able to keep you from stumbling,

And to present you faultless before the presence of His glory with exceeding joy,

To God our Savior,

Who alone is wise,

Be glory and majesty,

Dominion and power,

Both now and forever. Amen."

Jude 1:24-25

The crucible has done its work. The flame has found its rhythm. And now, the light must shine in your home, in your ministry, in every conversation and reconciliation. The world doesn't need perfect marriages; it needs purified ones. Homes where the Spirit dwells, hearts that love deeply, and flames that don't flicker at the first wind. You carry that flame now, not for display, but for direction.

Hold it high. Keep it holy and let its warmth draw others to the same Refiner who made your love glow again. And when the journey is over, when the work is done, and the flame burns its last, may you and your spouse hear the only words that truly matter:

"... 'Well done, good and faithful servant... enter into the joy of your lord.'"
Matthew 25:23

That is success. That is the goal.
That is the finish line of every faithful heart.

Reflection Moment

"Lord, am I serving You in a way that honors both my calling and my covenant?"

Father, help me to serve You with order and love. Teach me to live and minister with heaven in view. Let my home be my first altar, my marriage my first ministry, and my life a testimony of Your grace - so that when all is done, we may finish well and see You face to face.

EPILOGUE

The Flame You Carry - A Lantern Still Burning

Every refining leaves a glow. The crucible does not end when the fire fades. The glow that remains is proof that grace is stronger than any flame. The God who refines is still the God who restores.

Dear reader,

If you have reached this page, it means you have walked through the fire not just in these chapters, but in your own life, too.

You have paused where others might have rushed, prayed where others might have quit, and allowed truth to meet you tenderly.

For that, I thank you.

This book was not written merely to teach about marriage; it was written to reveal the heart of the Refiner.

Because every home, every heart, and every covenant will one day face the heat that tests its foundation.

The Crucible of the Christian Lantern is not a punishment; it is a process.

It is God's way of drawing out the dross and revealing the gold.

It is the place where love grows roots, where faith learns silence, and where grace learns shape.

"But may the God of all grace, who called us to His eternal glory by Christ Jesus, after you have suffered a while, perfect, establish, strengthen, and settle you."

1 Peter 5:10

This verse has carried me through seasons of refining, as a wife, a mother, a minister, and a woman simply learning to trust God more deeply.

And I pray that as you have read these pages, the same God of grace has begun the work of strengthening and settling you, too.

To the Married Still in the Crucible

May your love be steady and strong. Not because it never shakes, but because it always returns to the altar. May you learn to listen, to forgive, and to laugh again. Marriage will not perfect you -but it will refine you. Let God complete His work in you first.

The same Refiner who shapes one heart prepares another. Stay in the refining.

The fire that burns today may be the same fire that binds tomorrow.

Every misunderstanding is an invitation to grace. Every conflict is a call to compassion.

The goal is not to win, but to become.

Not to prove your love, but to reveal His.

"And after you have suffered a little while, the God of all grace... restore, confirm, strengthen, and establish you."

1 Peter 5:10 (ESV)

When you choose prayer over pride, forgiveness over fear, and tenderness over tension, heaven leans close.

Your endurance is your worship. Your humility is your power.

Your union is your Ministry. Hold hands in the heat.

Keep tending your flame.

Wait well, and know that the covenant ahead will carry purpose, not just passion.

May your home carry a fragrance that reminds everyone who enters, "Christ dwells here."

To the Wounded

For many, marriage has been a place of both beauty and breaking.

The vows were made with sincerity, but the seasons became heavy.

Hearts that once laughed together now ache in silence.

Yet God sees every fracture. He gathers every tear as oil for your lamp.

He has not forgotten you, and He will not waste your pain.

"A bruised reed He will not break, and smoking flax He will not quench."

Matthew 12:20a

You may feel like your light has gone out, but in the Father's eyes, even the faintest ember still burns bright with hope.

Let Him breathe upon it again. You are not beyond repair; you are being restored.

To the Divorced and Heartbroken

Some fires separate what was never meant to be destroyed.

The enemy wants you to wear shame, but God wants you to wear grace.

The covenant may have broken, but you have not been cast away.

He still writes redemption into the ashes. He still calls you beloved.

Your name has not changed in His mouth.

"He heals the brokenhearted and binds up their wounds."

Psalm 147:3

There is life beyond what ended. There is healing beyond regret.

One day, you will look back and see that the same God who allowed the breaking also began the rebuilding.

To the Children of Broken Homes

You have carried questions you never spoke.

You have watched love fade and wondered if the Covenant can truly last.

But even in the ruins, God was nearby.

He is not only the God of parents; He is the Father of the fatherless, the Keeper of the wounded heart.

You are not destined to repeat what you saw -you are chosen to rebuild differently.

"When my father and my mother forsake me, then the Lord will take care of me."

Psalm 27:10

Do not define your future by the pain you came from, but by the light you now carry.

You are the new lantern; one God Himself will tend.

To the Waiting and the Single

The fire may not have come yet, but the preparation has begun.

Waiting is its own kind of crucible: unseen, quiet, but holy.

It is in waiting that God refines your desires and strengthens your spirit.

"For the vision is yet for an appointed time... though it tarries, wait for it."

Habakkuk 2:3a

You are not being delayed; you are being developed.

You are not missing out; you are being made ready.

When the time is right, you will find that the waiting itself was oil for your lamp.

Let Him complete the work in you, so that when love comes, it finds you whole, not half-healed.

God never gives unfinished vessels to His sons and daughters.

To Ministers and Intercessors

You are the keepers of sacred flame.

Your altar burns for nations, for marriages, for revival. And sometimes, it costs more than words can tell.

In secret, you have carried burdens others never saw.

In silence, you have wrestled with discouragement, wondering if the fire still matters.

But the Lord says, "Do not despise the hidden fire."

Every tear you have sown in intercession is oil.

Every midnight prayer keeps a lamp burning somewhere you may never see.

"The effective, fervent prayer of a righteous man avails much."

James 5:16

To the ministers: your first ministry is still your home. Do not lose your lantern in the name of your pulpit.

Tend the flame within before you reach for the one outside. The anointing that flows from intimacy will sustain the public fire.

To the intercessors: do not grow weary. Heaven still answers whispered prayers. The oil you carry keeps others from burning out.

The Lord remembers every flame.

To Every Reader

Wherever this book finds you, whether whole or healing, weary or waiting, may it remind you that your story still burns with purpose.

You have not gone too far. You have not fallen too hard.

The light of God still seeks you, still surrounds you, still lives within you.

Your life is the lantern through which His love shines.

Let it burn in forgiveness. Let it burn in faith. Let it burn in surrender.

"For it is God who works in you both to will and to do for His good pleasure."

Philippians 2:13

When you lift this light, others will see the path to home.

And when your own strength fades, His Spirit will tend the flame until you glow again.

You are part of the story, a living witness that the crucible is not the end, but the beginning of the glow.

The light still shines. The marriage still matters.

The story still unfolds because the God who refines is still the God who restores.

So, keep shining. Keep loving. Keep forgiving.
Keep choosing grace.

And when it feels like the flame is flickering, remember this promise:

"But may the God of all grace, who called you to His eternal glory by Christ Jesus, after you have suffered a while, perfect, establish, strengthen, and settle you."
1 Peter 5:10

He who called you will sustain you.
He who refined you will restore you.
And He who lit your flame will keep it burning.

You are the lantern now. Carry your light.
Let it guide others home.

Be that flicker. Let your story guide. Let your scars teach. Let your flame shine

---

Final Prayer

Father, thank You for the refining fire that shapes love into holiness.
Thank You for grace that covers, heals, and strengthens.
Let every home represented on these pages become a beacon of peace and faith.
Keep our flames burning with humility and hope.

And let every marriage, old or new, broken or healed, shine for Your glory.

In Jesus' name, Amen.

Colette Ajoku

POSTSCRIPT - "EVER BRIGHTER"

Dear Reader,

I believe you have felt the warmth of grace along the way.

This book was never meant to instruct from a distance. It was written from within the fire, with the prayer that every word would carry healing, hope, and light to hearts that need reminding: you are not alone, and your story is not over. Marriage is not easy. It is holy, and holiness is rarely easy. It demands surrender, patience, forgiveness, and faith that stretches beyond feeling. But I have learned this truth: where there is surrender, there will always be grace. Your crucible does not define you; it refines you. And what emerges from it is not who you were, but who God is shaping you to become.

Keep the flame of your lantern burning. Feed it with prayer, guard it with humility, and fuel it with grace. The world still needs light, and the Lantern of Christ still burns in you.

"But the path of the just is like the shining sun, that shines ever brighter unto the perfect day."

Proverbs 4:18

May your marriage, your home, your heart, and your faith reflect the beauty of His restoration.

With love and prayer,

Colette Ajoku

RECOMMENDED READING & REFERENCES

Works Cited

Kenneth E. Hagin, *Love: The Way to Victory.* Kenneth Hagin Ministries, 1975. p. 71.

Arome Osayi, *Choices.* Iron Pen Kalma Kraft Ltd, 2019. p. 46.

Oyiks Alfred, *My Secret Place Devotional.* Olixbranders, 2022. p. 312.

Arome Osayi, *Decimating Demonic Devices.* Iron Pen Kalma Kraft Ltd, 2022. p. 35.

David Yonggi Cho, *The Fourth Dimension: Combined Edition.* Bridge-Logos Publishers, 1979. p. 55.

E.W. Kenyon and Don Gossett, *The Power of Your Words Devotional.* Whitaker House, 2021. p. 135.

Watchman Nee. *Spiritual Discernment.* Christian Fellowship Publishers Inc., 2010. p. 69

David Guzik, *Enduring Word Bible Commentary.* Enduring Word Media, enduringword.com. Accessed 2025.

BOOK BLURB

Marriage is more than companionship; it is a crucible where faith, love, and character are refined by fire.

In The Crucible of the Christian Lantern, Colette Ajoku gently leads readers through the sacred journey of covenant love from joy to tension, from testing to transformation. Blending Scripture, pastoral wisdom, and lived experience, she reveals how God uses the challenges of marriage to purify the heart and restore His design.

This book speaks to singles, married couples, those in crisis, and those healing from loss. It is a call to let go, let God, and discover that after the fire, there is still grace.

"You will not leave the crucible empty. You will leave it shining."

CONTACT SECTION

For ministry or book inquiries:

coletteajoku@gmail.com

Instagram: @coletteajoku

Impactville

Facebook: Colette Ajoku

www.ingramcontent.com/pod-product-compliance
Lightning Source LLC
LaVergne TN
LVHW010623100826
845148LV00014B/3087
* 9 7 8 9 7 8 6 9 1 9 8 2 9 *